STARTING GEOGRAPHY

Journeys

Written by
Helen Barden

Illustrated by
Robert Wheeler

Wayland

Books in the series

Clothes and Costumes	Landscapes
Conservation	Resources
Houses and Homes	Water
Journeys	Weather and Climate

First published in 1992 by
Wayland (Publishers) Ltd
61 Western Road, Hove
East Sussex, BN3 1JD, England

© Copyright 1992 Wayland (Publishers) Ltd

Series editor: Mandy Suhr
Designer: Jean Wheeler
Consultants: Julie Warne and Lorraine Harrison

British Library Cataloguing in Publication Data

Barden, Helen
Journeys – (Starting geography)
I Title   II. Series
388

HARDBACK ISBN 0–7502–0342–0

PAPERBACK ISBN 0–7502–0799–X

Typeset by DP Press, Sevenoaks, Kent
Printed in Italy by Rotolito Lombarda, S.p.A., Milan
Bound in Belgium by Casterman S.A.

Contents

Making a journey   4
Everyday journeys   6
On the road   8
Journeys in the air   10
Journeys across water   12
Journeys underground   14
Travelling on the track   16
All around the world   18
Going to work   20
Journeys without roads   22
Making maps   24
Journeys through history   26
Lift off!   28

Glossary   30
Finding out more   31
Index   32

The words printed in **bold** are explained in the glossary.

Making a journey

Do you like making a **journey**? There are many different ways of **travelling**. You can travel by foot, by car or by bus. You might even travel in a cart pulled by a donkey!

Some journeys are short. Others are much longer and might take you far away. Sometimes we make the same journey every day, maybe to go to work or to go to school.

◄ Sometimes journeys are exciting, like going on holiday. Other journeys may be difficult and dangerous, like those made by refugees, during a war or a famine.

Talk about the kinds of journeys you have made this week. How many different ways have you travelled?

Everyday journeys

Many people start the day by making a journey. These children in Haiti are going to school. What do you think they might pass along the way? ▶

These children in the USA are also on their way to school. They are travelling on a school bus. ▼

Ask your friends how they come to school. Who has the longest journey and who has the shortest journey?

Activity

How do you get to school? Can you draw a **map** to show your journey?

On the road

▲ Most everyday journeys are made along roads. They are built so that cars and trucks can travel around easily. Motorbikes and bicycles also travel along roads.

Roads are used to **transport** food and goods from place to place, as well as people. ▼

Think about the journeys you make on roads. Make a list of the different reasons for the journeys you make.

Some roads are large and busy. Others are quiet, narrow **lanes**. Special long, wide roads are built for long journeys. They have different names in different countries. In Britain they are called motorways. In the USA they are called freeways. This freeway is in Los Angeles.

Journeys in the air

Have you ever travelled by air? Aeroplanes and helicopters can travel long distances very quickly because they can go much faster than ships, cars or trains.

Many of us travel by air when we are going on a long journey. These children are going on holiday to another country. ▶

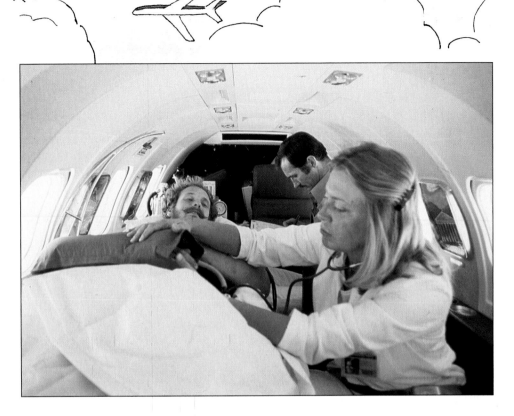

In parts of some countries, like Australia, there are not many roads, and towns and cities are very far apart. Aeroplanes and helicopters are used to take people and supplies to and from these towns. Doctors may have to fly all over the **outback** to visit their patients because they live so far apart. ▲

Activity

Have you ever travelled by aeroplane? Where did you go?
How long did your journey take? Try to find your **destination** on a map or a globe.

Journeys across water

Have you ever been on a boat? Did you travel on the sea or down a river? When people first began to explore the world, they made long journeys by boat to look for new lands. Now there are many different ways of travelling across water.

▲ Ships with big engines carry **cargo** from country to country. Passenger ferries carry people and cars across the sea to visit other countries. ▶

This **hovercraft** moves easily across the water of the English Channel.

These fishermen in Norway travel across the sea to fish. Their journeys may last many days and can be dangerous in rough seas.

Journeys underground

Sometimes a road or railway may have to be built through a mountain or under the ground, so a **tunnel** is built. Some tunnels are quite short but others can be very long.

▲ Some people have to travel underground to get to work. These coal miners are riding on special electric trains deep under the ground.

Lots of big cities all over the world have underground railways. These take people around the city much more quickly than by travelling on the busy roads. This train runs under the city of Paris, in France. ▶

Travelling on the track

All these people in China are using the railway to travel to work. Trains can carry many **passengers** at once. They are a fast way of travelling from place to place. ▶

Trains are also used to transport goods around the country. The Canadian Pacific railway line runs right across Canada. Some of the **freight trains** are over a kilometre long and need three **locomotives** to pull them. ▼

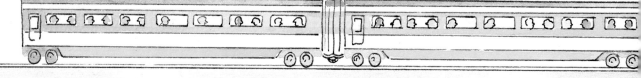

▲ The 'bullet train' in Japan is one of the fastest trains in the world.

Trams, like this one in Romania run on tracks on the road. There used to be lots of them in Britain, but now most of them have been replaced by buses. ▶

What is the name of your local railway station? Where do most of the trains go to?

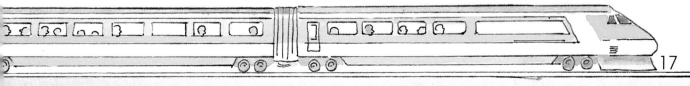

All around the world

Look at the traffic on the road. Many of the **vehicles** that you see are carrying goods from one place to another.

Some vehicles, like car transporters and petrol tankers are specially designed for the things they will carry. ▶

This tanker is full of milk. ▼

The aeroplane in this picture is designed to carry cargo from one country to another.

Many kinds of food have to be transported a long way. This breakfast cereal is grown in the USA and the sugar is grown in Jamaica. The oranges in the juice may have come from Spain and the coffee from Kenya.

Activity

Look at the labels on food tins and jars. Use a globe to help you find out where the food has come from. Which foods have made the longest journey?

Going to work

Some people make journeys all the time because of their work. This **pilot's** job is to fly people around in a helicopter. Taxi drivers, bus drivers and train drivers all travel around as part of their job.

These **trishaw** drivers in Indonesia take people from place to place.▼

This truck driver travels very long distances taking goods in her truck across the USA.

Activity

Imagine you are a pilot. Plan a journey that you must make in your aeroplane. Use a map of the world to help you. What is the reason for your journey?

Journeys without roads

In some places, animals are often used to transport goods and people. This may be because the landscape makes it too difficult to build good roads. Also, road building costs a great deal of money which some countries cannot afford.

In some desert areas, camels are used to carry people and goods. Camels can travel a long way without water. ▶

Sometimes people, like these women in India, have to move heavy loads. They may carry things on their backs or heads. They travel by foot where it would be difficult to drive a car or truck. ▼

Making maps

Have you ever looked at a map to find a **route**? Maps are very important because they show us which way to go.

A map is a drawing that shows the shape of the land and the things that are there. Different kinds of maps can give different kinds of information. There are maps of most parts of the world. Some maps are designed to show where roads and motorways are. These maps can help us to plan a route for a journey.

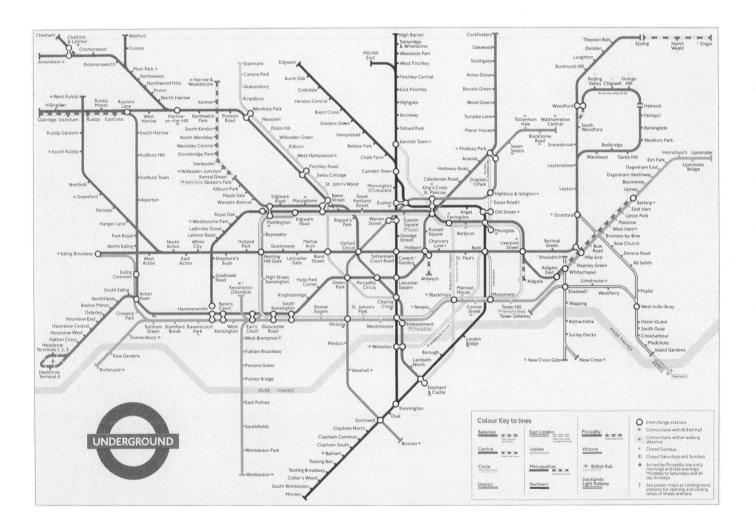

▲ This is a map of the London underground railway, in Britain. Can you spot Victoria station? Plan a route from Victoria station to Camden Town station. Use the key to help you.

Use a large scale map to plan a route around your local area. Can you find your school? What other buildings can you see on the map?

Journeys through history

▲ Today, many people travel all over the world. It is quite easy to get from place to place. Before roads, railways and aeroplanes were built, travelling was much slower. People travelled on foot or by **wagon**. The people in this picture travelled many hundreds of kilometres across the plains of the USA, in the days of the early settlers. The journeys were long and dangerous. ▼

As journeys took so much longer, fewer people were able to travel. To move around Europe meant long, slow journeys by horseback or by coach, that could be very uncomfortable. ▼

▲ Now there are lots of different ways to travel around, such as on this **monorail**, in the USA. How many different kinds of modern transport can you find out about?

Lift off!

Today, people have even travelled into space. Rockets have been built so that people can explore the other planets and stars in our universe.

Can you imagine walking on the moon? In 1969, two Americans landed on the moon. Since then **astronauts** from other countries have also been to the moon.

The first journey into space was made by a Russian dog called Laika. Now astronauts travel out into space and live in space stations for many weeks.

What do you think the earth would look like from space?

Activity

Imagine you are making a space journey. Design your own spacecraft. Draw the things that you would need to take with you.

Glossary

Astronaut   A person who travels into space.

Cargo   The goods that a ship, plane or lorry carries.

Destination   The place at the end of your journey.

Freight train   A train that transports goods not people.

Hovercraft   A vehicle that travels on a cushion of air across land and water.

Journey   A trip from one place to another.

Lanes   Narrow roads.

Locomotives   Engines that pull trains along a track.

Map   An accurate drawing that shows the shape of a place and the things that are there.

Monorail   A single-track railway that is often built on stilts.

Outback   The bush country of Australia.

Passengers   People travelling in a vehicle.

Pilot   The person who flies an aeroplane.

Route   The way that you decide to go when you want to go somewhere.

Trams   Vehicles that run on rails over a road to carry passengers around a place.

Transport   To take or carry something from place to place.

Travelling   Going from one place to another.

Trishaw   A three-wheeled passenger vehicle used like a taxi.

Tunnel   A passageway built underground or through a hill or mountain.

Vehicles   Machines that move, usually with wheels.

Wagon   A vehicle with four wheels pulled along by horses.

Finding out more

Books to read

Space Voyages by Norman Barrett (Franklin Watts, 1990)

Transport Machines by Norman Barrett (Franklin Watts, 1991)

On My Way To School by Celia Berridge (Andre Deutsch, 1985)

The Journey Home by Joanne Flindall (Walker Books, 1988)

Look Around Transport by Clive Pace and Jean Birch (Wayland, 1989)

Let's Look at Aircraft by Andrew Langley (Wayland, 1989)

Let's Look at Trains by Andrew Langley (Wayland, 1988)

Let's Look at Ships and Boats by Rupert Matthews (Wayland, 1989)

Paths, Streets and Motorways by Henry Pluckrose (Blackwell, 1989)

Truck Driver by Tim Wood, (Franklin Watts, 1989)

Picture acknowledgements

The photographs in this book were supplied by: Cephas 13 (above), 22 (below); Chapel Studios 17 (below), 25; Bruce Coleman Ltd 6 (above), 18 (centre), 22 (above); David Cumming COVER; Ecoscene 8, 20 (below), Hutchinson 16 (below); Photri 18 (above), 20 (above), 21; Peter Newark's Western Americana 26, 27; Science Photo Library 28 (inset); Tony Stone Worldwide 4, 6 (below), 9, 12 (below), 13 (below), 15 (above), 16 (above), 17 (above), 18 (below), 23 (below), 26, 27, 29 (above); Topham 15 (below); TRH 28; Wayland 5 (above), 7, 12 (above), 24; Zefa 5 (below), 10, 11.

Index

Aeroplane   4, 10, 11, 18, 21, 26
Animals   22
Astronauts   28
Atlas   19
Australia   11

Bicycles   8
Boat   12
   passenger ferries   12
   ship   10, 12

Camels   23
Canada   16
Car   4, 8, 10, 23
   car transporter   18

Deserts   23

Flying doctor   11
Food   19

Globe   11

Haiti   6
Helicopter   11, 10
Holiday   5
Hovercraft   13

India   23
Indonesia   20

Jamaica   19
Japan   17

Kenya   19

Map   7, 11, 24, 25
Milk tanker   18
Moon   28
Motorbike   8

Norway   13

Pilot   20

Railway   10, 14, 16, 17, 26
   bullet train   17
   Canadian Pacific Railway   16
   electric trains   15
   monorail   27
   underground railway   18
Refugees   5
Roads   8, 9, 11, 14, 15, 22, 25, 26
   freeway   9
   motorway   9
Rocket   28
Route   24, 25

School   6, 7
Space   28, 29
   space station   29
Spain   19

Tram   17
Trishaw   19
Truck   8, 23
Tunnel   14

USA   6, 9, 19, 21, 26